MW01268343

WILDLIFE
OF
YELLOWSTONE
AND
GRAND TETON
NATIONAL PARKS

M. Douglas Scott, Ph.D.
and
Suvi A. Scott, M.S.

Wheelwright Publishing
Helena, Montana

ACKNOWLEDGMENTS

The publisher would like to acknowledge the assistance of Sharlene Milligan and the Grand Teton Natural History Association and the staff of Grand Teton National Park in the preparation of *Wildlife of Yellowstone and Grand Teton National Parks.* Thank you also to Yellowstone National Park staff for their cooperation.

All photos courtesy of Grand Teton National Park
unless otherwise noted.

Drawings by Bryan Harry
Former Assistant Chief Naturalist
Yellowstone National Park

Front Cover—Rocky Mountain Elk
Photo by Carol Polich
©Carol Polich/circumerrostock.com

INTRODUCTION

Sometimes it seems that all the earthly frontiers of exploration are gone—that it is next to impossible to do or learn anything original. A thousand years hence, however, our descendants may look upon us with envy. We live in a time when really very little is known about the natural world around us. It is our good fortune to be discovering new knowledge about those other life forms which have lived, and developed, on earth alongside humanity. Even though many wild animals are fairly easy to find and observe, we are hardly well-acquainted. For some, it is possible to learn all that is known about their life histories after reading for only a few days. The person who examines just two or three selections from the reference list in this book will quickly find huge gaps in knowledge for any given animal, even though these books are quite detailed. Often, "facts" do not agree. How acute *really* is the eyesight of a grizzly bear? What is the true use and meaning of sounds made by red squirrels? How do Clark's nutcrackers survive cold winter nights?

It is clear that a frontier, and thus a little bit of Man's heritage, is lost if an animal is exterminated. Even if a once-abundant animal is kept alive in a zoo, or in some small refuge, the loss is great because there is no way of knowing how it lived when spread out in a wide variety of natural environments—not to mention the loss in genetic diversity when most of a species has been killed off. For great parks like Grand Teton and Yellowstone, one of their most important contributions is that they preserve wild animals under conditions which are reasonably similar to those in which the animals have been evolving. Thus, the parks offer humanity the chance to see, to study, and to appreciate the complex lives of our fellow creatures under the most natural conditions possible. We hope that this book will give park visitors new insights into the lives of our Rocky Mountain animals, and that this knowledge will result in even greater understanding of the need for park preservation for all time.

3

Pika

HABITAT

People interested in nature often hear or read that all animals need sufficient "habitat" in order to survive. This somewhat pretentious word is made a lot easier to understand when it is translated. It simply means "home." The most important characteristics of a land animal's home are the kinds of plant communities that exist there. Herbivorous (plant-eating) animals, such as deer, need the right mix of plant types for adequate nutrition and, in turn, carnivorous (meat-eating) animals depend upon the plant eaters for meat. When weather conditions become extreme, plants provide animals with shade from the hot sun or a screen against fierce winter snowstorms.

Over the course of time, many kinds of plants have evolved to take advantage of the many environments available to them—from desert sands to lake shores. When a variety of plant types grow together in a similar environment, it is termed a plant community. In turn, animals have evolved different forms which can take advantage of the various plant communities. Some animals, like the sage grouse or pronghorn, are largely restricted to certain plant communities, while others, like the raven or black bear, are quite versatile and seem to do best when they have a choice of many communities.

One of the reasons that Yellowstone and Grand Teton National Parks are such a haven for wildlife is that this large area (over 2.5 million acres) provides a wide range of environments for plant communities. Elevations range from less than 5,200 feet in the north end of Yellowstone near Stephens Creek, to 13,770 feet at the summit of the Grand Teton. Numerous mountains in both parks are over 10,000 feet high. Precipitation averages less than 12 inches per year in the semi-arid Stephens Creek area to over 70 inches on the flanks of the higher mountains. The various combinations of environmental factors give rise to ten major plant community types. These types, and some of the animals featured in this book that are associated with them, are given below.

Streamside (Riparian) Vegetation. Willows, cottonwoods, and grass-like sedges dominate this community. Soils are rich and often waterlogged. Willows provide food and construction material for beavers, and great blue herons build stick nests in the tall cottonwoods.

Lowland Pond and Marsh Vegetation. Shallow, quiet ponds develop thick beds of organic muck, and this supports a luxuriant growth of sedges, grasses, and smartweeds along the pond margins. Toward the center, the pond may produce aquatic plants like rushes and pondweeds. Such plants make a delectable salad for moose, trumpeter swans, and the many kinds of ducks that frequent these areas.

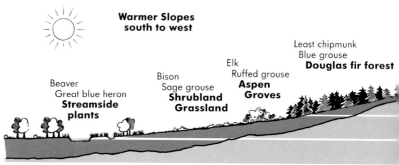

Warmer Slopes south to west

Least chipmunk
Blue grouse
Douglas fir forest

Elk
Ruffed grouse
Aspen Groves

Bison
Sage grouse
Shrubland Grassland

Beaver
Great blue heron
Streamside plants

Generalized vegetation types in Yellowstone and Grand Teton National Parks.

Mixed Grasses and Shrubs. The large flats and low rolling hills of northern Yellowstone and southern and eastern Grand Teton support broad expanses of rangeland composed of grasses and shrubs. Pronghorns and sage grouse feed extensively on the big sage plants that grow in these areas. Bison relish the wheatgrass, fescue, and needlegrass found on the dry plains.

Aspen Groves. Small colonies of aspens, ranging in size from a few trees to stands ten acres in size or more, can be found scattered here and there in the two parks. They may occur as isolated clumps in shrub-grass range or may be intermingled with Douglas fir on steeper hillsides. Their presence usually indicates that the site is wetter than nearby soils. Elk are fond of nibbling at the small "sucker" shoots which aspens produce. Ruffed grouse may browse on aspen buds in winter and often feast on the wild strawberries which grow in and around the more open stands in summer.

Lodgepole Pine Forest. The presence of a thick stand of lodgepole pines usually indicates that a site experienced a forest fire sometime within the last 200-300 years. These opportunistic trees establish themselves easily on almost any place where bare mineral soil has been exposed, but they seem to do the very best on large, gently sloping plateaus at medium elevations. The globe huckleberry is a typical shrub that grows rank under lodgepole pines, and this is a favorite hiding place of the snowshoe hare. In late summer, gray jays and bears may be seen searching the bushes for the tasty, dark purple berries.

Douglas Fir Forest. Douglas firs are versatile trees and can grow on fairly wet to quite dry sites. In the wetter locations, this kind of forest is gradually replaced by spruce-fir forests. On dry sites, however, Douglas firs may reproduce successfully and maintain their dominance indefinitely. Often, Douglas firs are found in clumps intermingled with grass-forb meadows, and it seems to be an ongoing battle as to which plant community will take over the site. This war zone

6

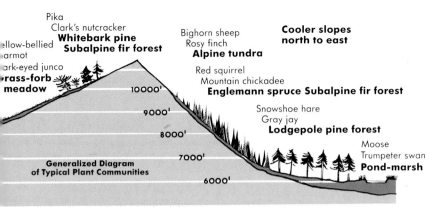

Pika
Clark's nutcracker
Whitebark pine
Subalpine fir forest

Yellow-bellied marmot
Dark-eyed junco
Grass-forb meadow

Bighorn sheep
Rosy finch
Alpine tundra

Cooler slopes north to east

Red squirrel
Mountain chickadee
Englemann spruce Subalpine fir forest

Snowshoe hare
Gray jay
Lodgepole pine forest

Moose
Trumpeter swan
Pond-marsh

10000'
9000'
8000'
7000'
6000'

Generalized Diagram of Typical Plant Communities

Examples of wildlife found in these habitats.

is ideal, however, for the least chipmunk and blue grouse, who both need protection provided by trees, as well as food from the meadows.

Spruce-Fir Forest. In this part of the Rocky Mountains, the Englemann spruce and subalpine fir are the trees that eventually become dominant on most forest sites that are not extremely dry or rocky. In the absence of fire, these trees will form a thick, dark canopy over the ground and shade out many plants that are used as food by various animals. Nevertheless, the red squirrel relishes the seed-bearing cones from the trees, and the mountain chickadee ranges through the gloomy woods, searching for tiny insect treasures within the furrowed bark.

Grass-Forb Meadows. At some moderately high elevations where soils are better developed, grasses and herbaceous plants (forbs) seem to get the upper hand over the surrounding forest. These places make ideal pastures for the yellow-bellied marmot, and dark-eyed juncos can always try to find seeds scattered among the plant stems.

Whitebark Pine-Subalpine Fir Forest. The highest, coldest, rockiest, and windiest places that trees can grow in the Central Rockies are inhabited by tough whitebark pines and a few stunted subalpine firs. The Clark's nutcracker likes to pry the big whitebark pine nuts out of their cones, and the pika is sequestered in the many rockslides which tumble through these scattered groves of trees.

Alpine Tundra. The treeline in Yellowstone and Grand Teton is about 9,500-10,000 feet in elevation. Above this, forests give way to short grasses and forbs which are able to withstand freezing, summer drought, gales, intense sunlight, and months of being buried under several feet of snow. Most animals only visit such places for a short time in the summer. The bighorn sheep is a common summer grazer here, and the rosy finch often chooses such an unlikely place to obtain insect food.

THE MAMMALS

Animals that have hair and provide milk to their newborn young are called mammals. This book deals with those larger mammals that are readily seen along roadsides or during short hikes in the backcountry. Naturally, park visitors should not attempt to closely approach large mammals like bears, moose, or bison. Smaller animals should not be fed or touched. For aspiring mammalogists, a complete list of all mammal species is provided in the appendix.

Black Bear. The most common bear that might be seen in the parks is the black bear, which is about 30 inches high and usually weighs between 150-250 pounds. Surprisingly, about half the black bears in this part of the country are not black; many are a light brown, cinnamon, or even blond color. The mother bear usually gives birth to two cubs every other year, and it is not unusual for the cubs to be two different colors. Although both young and adult black bears can easily climb trees to safety, the female is likely to be aggressive toward any person who gets too close to the cubs. Bears are seldom seen along park roads. However, the vigilant backcountry traveler might encounter these animals almost anywhere in the parks, especially in the narrow canyons in the southwestern part of Grand Teton or in the small valleys of northwestern Yellowstone.

Grizzly Bear. Grizzly bears have brown coats, and the hair tips may be whitish or silvery, producing a "grizzled" look. Grizzlies are larger than black bears, weighing 300-600 pounds or more, and they have a noticeable hump over their front shoulders. In profile, the grizzly has a concave, dished-out face. The claws of grizzlies are longer and straighter than those of black bears but, contrary to popular opinion, this does not prevent adult grizzlies from climbing trees. Like black bears, grizzlies undergo a partial hibernation between November and April, but during the rest of the year, they may turn up at almost any place in Yellowstone or the northwestern corner of Grand Teton. For obvious safety reasons, park visitors

Black bear
Photo: Diana Stratton

Sow black bear and cubs
Photo: Diana Stratton

Grizzly bear and cub
Photo: Jess R. Lee

should never attempt to search for grizzly bears. Some areas of Yellowstone are closed to human entry during summer months, both for the protection of humans and the prevention of disturbance to this rare animal.

Coyote. The coyote is an intelligent, wary animal and, in most parts of this country, is difficult to view for more than a few seconds. This shyness results from nearly universal persecution of coyotes by trappers, farmers, and hunters, who sometimes believe that coyotes do more damage to livestock and wildlife than actually is the case. In reality, the major foods of this small, 25-pound, wild dog are ground squirrels, jack rabbits, carrion, and a variety of vegetable matter. In winter and early spring coyotes may be seen hunting on the Antelope Flats of eastern Grand Teton and in the Lamar Valley of Yellowstone. Later, in April or May, the female coyote will give birth to five or six pups, tucked away safely in an underground den, like an old badger burrow. By late summer, the pups accompany their parents on hunts, and the high-pitched chorus of wails, yips, and howls produced by the temporary pack is a campfire song long remembered by back-country campers.

Gray Wolf. In early spring a mated wolf pair digs an underground den. This is used by the female as a place to give birth to three to seven pups. Pups are old enough to fend for themselves when a year old but may stay with the parents, thus forming the nucleus of a pack. During the first part of the 20th century, gray wolves were eliminated from the greater Yellowstone area. This was done because government agencies were convinced that wolves were a threat to the survival of other wildlife. In recent years, wolves have been reintroduced into Yellowstone and Grand Teton from Canada. Within a short time they have established numerous packs throughout the parks and the greater Yellowstone ecosystem. The Lamar Valley is a good place to observe one of these packs.

Coyote

Coyote pup

Gray wolves

Red Fox. The coyote may prey on red foxes so, in the two parks, foxes are not highly abundant. This beautiful 10-15 pound animal usually sports a reddish brown coat with a white-tipped tail, but other, very different, color phases may occur. One such color phase is the cross fox, which has a dark cross-shaped pattern over its shoulders and down the back. This animal is quite rare. An excellent place to see the cross fox is on the open slopes of Mount Washburn in Yellowstone. Red foxes sometimes den in a marmot burrow. After the five or six young foxes are born in April or May, the parents feed them a variety of small prey, including mice, frogs, snowshoe hares, and birds.

Long-tailed Weasel. Long-tailed weasels are dark brown in summer and turn white in winter. This adaptation provides seasonal camouflage when stalking prey or avoiding predators, as the situation dictates. Favorite foods of the weasel are mice, voles, bird eggs, and insects. This small carnivore produces a single litter of six to nine young per year. After about two months, the young leave the nest to lead solitary lives.

Striped Skunk. Possibly excepting the badger, the striped skunk is the least weasel-like animal in the weasel family. However, like other members of this group, the skunk possesses strong-smelling musk glands. The skunk has developed musk to its foulest perfection and is able to spray the concoction into an enemy's eyes 10 feet away or more. Since the skunk is so well armed, it is an advantage to advertise the fact to potential predators. Unlike most land mammals, the skunk does not wear protective camouflage but, instead, has a striking black and white pelt. Striped skunks prefer the lower elevation sagebrush-grassland areas of northern Yellowstone and southeastern Grand Teton, where they can hunt mice, insects, bird eggs, and carrion. They also seem to be attracted to shorelines, and visitors to campgrounds along Jackson Lake or the Gros Ventre River have a good chance of seeing a skunk out on an evening foraging expedition.

Red fox

Long-tailed weasel   Photo: Ray O. Kirkland

Striped skunk

Photo:
Ray O.
Kirkland

River Otter. Adult river otters weigh from 10 to 30 pounds and are three to four feet long, including the tail. These highly aquatic mammals live in lakes and larger streams. They may be seen along the Madison River in Yellowstone and at Oxbow Bend in Grand Teton. Otters build an underground den in the lake or stream bank, and it has entrances both above and below water. The litter of two or three young otters is born in April. At about three months old, the young begin hunting fish with the mother.

Mountain Lion. Mountain lions are also called cougars. Except for the jaguar, this is the largest member of the cat family in North America, with adults weighing 125-200 pounds. Mountain lions feed mainly on other large mammals like deer and elk but also will kill porcupines, rabbits, and grouse. Female lions may produce a litter almost any month of the year, and the two kittens are usually kept in a cave or under a rock pile. Young leave the mother when they are about two years old, and she then has a new litter. Mountain lions are cautious, shy animals, but they may occasionally be seen in the Lizard Creek area of Grand Teton or along the Black Canyon stretch of the Yellowstone River.

Rocky Mountain Elk. The "off-season," during fall and winter, is one of the best times of the year to see wildlife in the parks. At this time, it would be almost impossible for a visitor not to see a Rocky Mountain elk. In September, bulls move near Yellowstone's lower Gardner River for the breeding season, and their piercing "bugle" (which is more like a loud whistle) can be heard throughout the area around Mammoth Hot Springs. In Jackson Hole, visitors can observe thousands of wintering elk on the National Elk Refuge, which extends from Jackson to the southern edge of Grand Teton. Elk, or wapiti as they are sometimes called, migrate from throughout the park to the refuge every autumn. During the summer, travelers to Old Faithful may frequently see elk in the Fountain Flats area, especially in the early morning or late afternoon. In Grand Teton, the sagebrush-grassland area east of Jenny Lake can be a productive place to find elk.

River otters   Photo: Diana Stratton

Mountain lion   Photo: Jess R. Lee

Bull elk bugling   Photo: Diana Stratton

Mule Deer. Besides having larger ears, mule deer generally are somewhat heavier than typical white-tailed deer, which are scarce in the two parks. "Muley" bucks will often weigh 200-275 pounds while does are 50-100 pounds lighter. At least a few mule deer can be seen almost anywhere in the parks. In Yellowstone, the best place to observe them is around the North Entrance near Gardiner, Montana. In Grand Teton, wooded areas surrounding the Colter Bay and Lizard Creek campgrounds are good places to find mule deer during summer. In the evening, does and fawns may be seen foraging through open lodgepole pine forests and meadows, searching out favorite foods like serviceberry and honeysuckle leaves.

Shiras Moose. The Shiras moose is an unusually dark colored variety of moose, and this animal evidently has only resided in the parks for about 150 years. Before then, trappers and explorers seldom saw moose in the mountains of Idaho, Montana, or Wyoming. Moose seem to be everywhere in Grand Teton, but two of the most reliable places to see them are the Willow Flats area southwest of Jackson Lake Lodge or the Buffalo Fork willow thickets on the eastern park boundary. Moose are not as abundant in Yellowstone, but often may be found along the Yellowstone River in Hayden Valley or in willow bottoms near Indian Creek campground. The moose is the largest member of the deer family. Mature bulls may weigh 900 pounds or more, and cows average around 600-800 pounds.

Gray wolf

Mule deer and twin fawns Photo: Diana Stratton

Bull elk in velvet Photo: Diana Stratton

Shiras bull moose Photo: Jeff Foott

Pronghorn. Unlike other North American hoofed mammals, the pronghorn has no fossil ancestors on other continents—at least for many millions of years back. Therefore, it is not closely related to the true antelopes of Africa and southeast Asia, although our pronghorn is popularly called an "antelope." America's fastest land mammal, the adult pronghorn is capable of sprinting 45-50 miles per hour. The twin pronghorn fawns can walk within 30 minutes after birth and can run 10-20 miles per hour after two or three days. Like other members of their family, pronghorns have horns, but they differ in that the horn is forked, and it is shed every year, in late autumn. Pronghorns are open range-sagebrush and grassland loving animals. At all times of the year, they can be seen in Yellowstone along the gravel road north of the Roosevelt Arch, near Gardiner, Montana. In Grand Teton, pronghorns may be observed on Antelope Flats and Baseline Flat, east and north of the park headquarters at Moose.

Cow moose with calf Photo: Diana Stratton

Pronghorn (antelope) Photo: Diana Stratton

Pronghorn herd Photo: Jess R. Lee

Bison. The bison (American buffalo) were once the most numerous large mammals in North America, and it is the largest land mammal on the continent. It has been estimated that, at the beginning of the 18th century, the American plains supported 60 million of the 1,000-2,000 pound beasts. This animal is a part of our American heritage and language: the buffalo nickel; Buffalo Bill; or being "buffaloed" by someone. It seems almost poetic coincidence that America's first national park, Yellowstone, was the place the last wild buffalo in the U.S. were saved from slaughter. Even here, the herd dwindled to only about 50 before the U.S. Army was sent in 1886 to help protect the park animals from poachers. Today, the buffalo herd is healthy in Yellowstone, and they may be seen contentedly munching grass in the Hayden and Lamar Valleys. In Grand Teton, buffalo are often found in the Potholes area and along the Snake River.

Bighorn Sheep. In the spring and summer, bighorn sheep are not often seen by park visitors. These animals usually retreat to the high alpine tundra areas of the mountaintops during these seasons to rear their lambs and feed on lush new plant growth. Usually a single lamb is born to each adult ewe in April, and within a day or two the youngster is able to climb steep cliffs along with its mother. The highest parts of Mount Washburn and Mount Everts are typical sheep summering areas in Yellowstone, while Mount Hunt and Owl and Ranger Peaks in the Teton Range usually have a few residents. By far the best time and place to see and photograph bighorn sheep is in the winter, around the base of Mount Everts. Ewes, lambs, and even adult rams with massive full-curl horns can be seen daintily nibbling grass along the banks of the Gardner River, on the west side of the mountain.

Bison cow with calf   Photo: Robert Cooper
Bison bull   Photo: Janet Jahoda-Rogers

Bighorn rams   Photo: Diana Stratton

Least Chipmunk. A hiker traveling up to Grand View Point in Grand Teton National Park might be mildly startled to see a tiny orange and brown squirrel with "mumps" scurrying across the path just ahead. Chances are it was a least chipmunk, who just finished stuffing his cheek pouches full of seeds in one of the nearby dry grass-forb meadows. These rodents never seem to move slowly, and this one was probably rushing back to one of the large Douglas firs on the hillside. Once there, the little squirrel could deposit its grain treasure in a food cache hidden underneath one of the massive roots, safe from any passing jays. Like other chipmunks, the least chipmunk is sort of a cross between a ground squirrel and a tree squirrel. It does most of its foraging on the ground but often climbs up shrubs and small trees, searching for ripe berries or even seed from pine cones.

Yellow-bellied Marmot. There is hardly a canyon, mountainside, or cliff in the two parks that does not support at least a few yellow-bellied marmots. Anyplace that has large boulders and rockslides intermingled with lush mountain meadows is a potential marmot home. On mild, sunny days from March through August, marmots spend most of the time outside of their underground dens, carefully plucking and eating a variety of wild mountain flowers and alpine grasses. When disturbed, one or two marmots will sit upright and utter a loud whistle, which sends all nearby friends hurrying for their dens. Marmots are low-slung, five-to-ten-pound mammals, and are good diggers. By the time September snows arrive in the high mountains, the marmots retreat to their dens to hibernate. Before the snow melts in March, the marmots reappear, and shortly afterwards, the litter of four to six young is born.

Bighorn sheep   Photo: Diana Stratton

Least chipmunk   Photo: Janet Jahoda-Rogers

Yellow-bellied marmot   Photo: Robert Cooper

Uinta Ground Squirrel. At lower elevations in both parks, such as near developed campgrounds, along roadsides, and in the sagebrush flats, park visitors may hear a short, sharp squeak that resembles the marmot's call, but is not as loud or as long. If a person stands still for a few moments, he or she should soon spot one or more Uinta ground squirrels cautiously peeking above the edge of a three-inch wide burrow. Uinta ground squirrels emerge from underground hibernation in March or April and sometimes have to tunnel through one or two feet of snow to reach the surface. They search out early dandelions and grasses in the few bare patches and gradually expand their feeding grounds as the snow recedes. The young are born in May, when the snow is almost entirely gone. Uinta ground squirrels are active only a short part of the year. When the hot days of July and August arrive, the adults return to their burrows and begin estivation, which is a summer type of hibernation. Often, they pass directly from estivation to hibernation, so they may remain underground, without food or water, for eight to nine continuous months a year.

Golden-mantled Ground Squirrel. An outcrop of broken rock in a dry forest clearing is a promising location to look for golden-mantled ground squirrels. Typically, the entrance to a squirrel's burrow is hidden somewhere among the crevices or under a nearby shrub. Since these squirrels spend about half the year (October-April) in the deep sleep of hibernation, they are wise to conceal their burrows as much as possible from the attention of predators like the long-tailed weasel. Golden-mantled ground squirrels breed soon after emerging from hibernation, and the two to eight young are born in late May or early June. White and black stripes on the body of this ten-inch long ground squirrel make it look like an oversize chipmunk, but a lack of definite stripes on the face distinguishes it from its smaller cousins. Favorite foods of golden-mantled ground squirrels include seeds, leaves, buds, and roots, but animal foods like carrion and bird eggs may also be consumed.

Yellow-bellied marmots Photo: Diana Stratton
Uinta ground squirrel Photo: Janet Jahoda-Rogers

Golden-mantled ground squirrel Photo: Janet Jahoda-Rogers

Red Squirrel. It is a little ironic that the large, fierce grizzly bear sometimes depends upon the small red squirrel to gather its food. In years when the whitebark pine trees produce abundant fertile cones, each red squirrel will cut thousands of cones off the branches and hide them in an underground cache for consumption during winter. When a bear happens to smell the cones with their sweet nuts inside it generally unearths and consumes the whole cache, leaving nothing for the hard-working squirrel. Bears do this so commonly that biologists believe a year with a good whitebark pine nut crop will be good for grizzly populations.

Beaver. As evidenced by its large gnawing teeth, the beaver is a rodent—the largest rodent in North America. Beavers have been known to cut down trees up to two feet in diameter in only one or two night's work. These animals eat bark from the fallen trees, with favorites being aspen, cottonwood, and willow. The well-known beaver dam is an amazing example of how simple materials like sticks, mud, and gravel can be arranged by an animal into a product that is watertight enough to form a small pond. Once the pond is built, the beavers build a lodge in it that has safe underwater entrances. It is here that the usually four or five beaver kits are born. An excellent place to see beavers in Grand Teton is at Heron Pond or Swan Lake. Beaver numbers have declined in Yellowstone, but they still may be readily observed along the Gallatin River, on the park's west boundary.

Mink

Red squirrel   Photo: Eddie Bowman
Beaver   Photo: Jackie Gilmore

Beaver   Photo: Jackie Gilmore

Muskrat and lodge

Muskrat. American rats and mice come in lots of sizes, but the muskrat is the biggest one of all, weighing three to four pounds. These are semi-aquatic mammals, and lowland marshes or slow-moving streams are their favorite haunts. Muskrats eat all kinds of aquatic plants, including sedges, rushes, cattails, and smartweeds. Cattails and rushes also are a favorite item used by muskrats to build their four-to-five-foot-high cone-shaped houses. The houses, or sometimes underground bank dens, are birthplaces for the several litters of five or six young produced every summer. Muskrat houses may be seen on Christian Pond, just east of Jackson Lake Lodge in Grand Teton. In Yellowstone, they can be observed on the Blacktail Ponds, which are between Mammoth Hot Springs and Tower Junction.

Porcupine. Most people are aware that the porcupine is covered with sharp quills with which to ward off enemies. However, it is not true that porcupines can throw their quills with a flick of their tail. Having adequate self-defense equipment, porcupines are very slow movers. In summer, they emerge from makeshift dens at nightfall and slowly graze their way through meadow stands of clover, lupine, grasses, and low shrubs. In winter, the porcupine's diet shifts almost exclusively to tree bark. A person walking through almost any lodgepole pine forest in Yellowstone or Grand Teton will see evidence of the porcupine's appetite. Many trees will have large patches of yellow wood covered with white sap, and those trees that have been completely girdled are doomed to die.

Muskrat

Porcupine   Photo: Jackie Gilmore

Porcupine   Photo: Eddie Bowman

Pika. The six-inch pika is related to rabbits and, indeed, is sometimes called a "rock rabbit." Ordinarily, pikas are quite shy and quickly duck out of sight back into rockslide dens at the approach of a human. On the heavily used Cascade Canyon and Paintbrush Canyon trails in Grand Teton, pikas may stay out and allow an opportunity for a good photograph. Pikas do not hibernate in winter, even though their rock pile nests may be buried under several feet of snow. They are able to survive because they cut and dry a variety of forbs and grasses during the summer and then feed on their "haystacks" all winter long.

Snowshoe Hare. During late evenings in the summer, campers in forested parts of the parks have a good chance of seeing timid snowshoe hares quietly hopping about, looking for choice morsels of clover or huckleberry. At this time of the year, the hares are a dull brownish gray, and they blend well with their forest surroundings. Hares give birth to two separate litters of one to seven young each summer, and the young are able to run and hide only minutes after being born. As winter approaches, the snowshoe hare gradually turns completely white, except for a small amount of black on its ears. Also, the hairs on the animal's hind feet grow longer, and it is then equipped with "snowshoes," as well as camouflage, when trying to escape predators after snow covers the forest.

White-tailed Jack Rabbit. Unlike the snowshoe hare, the white-tailed jack rabbit lives in open country. Sagebrush-grassland range seems to be preferred by this animal, and sagebrush is an important part of its annual diet. In the summer, the jack rabbit also consumes a variety of forbs and grasses. This large hare does not build a permanent nest but simply scrapes out a shallow bowl-shaped "form" for a temporary resting place. Several such forms may be used within the jack rabbit's home range. The litter of three or four young is born in one of these forms in May or June. White-tailed jack rabbits are especially abundant in the Stephens Creek area of Yellowstone and are occasionally found in the sagebrush flats south of Moose, in Grand Teton National Park.

Pika   Photo: Jackie Gilmore

Snowshoe hare   Photo: Jess R. Lee

White-tailed jack rabbit   Photo: Kathrina Buechner

**Overleaf, Grand Canyon
of the Yellowstone,**
photo by L.F. Wheelwright

THE BIRDS

Birds are warm-blooded animals that have feathers. There are nearly four times as many birds as mammals in the two parks, partly because far more birds than mammals are just seasonal residents. As with the mammals, only the larger, common birds which are easily recognizable by most park visitors are described.

American White Pelican. Flashing their large white bodies and black wingtips, a flock of white pelicans wheeling high in the air over Yellowstone or Jackson Lakes looks like a flock of snow geese at first glance. Then, lowering for the landing, the enormous orange bill with the large pouch becomes evident, and there is no doubt as to the birds' identity. When not fishing in the shallow parts of these lakes, pelicans may be found on the Yellowstone River not far below the lake, or on Oxbow Bend of the Snake River, in Grand Teton. Pelicans nest on the small Molly Islands in the Southeast Arm of Yellowstone Lake. To avoid disturbing them, boats are not allowed within one-quarter mile of the islands. When the two or three eggs hatch in the mound-shaped nest, both parents assist in feeding the young a "soup" of regurgitated fish.

Great Blue Heron. Visitors to the larger streams in the parks, like the Madison River in Yellowstone or the Snake River in Grand Teton, are bound to see a stately great blue heron before too long. The four-foot-high bird stands quietly in the shallows, waiting to suddenly spear a passing fish or frog with its long, dagger-shaped bill. When disturbed, the bird ponderously leaps into the air, utters a loud, hoarse croak, and flaps away. Flying herons are sometimes mistaken for cranes, but they are easy to tell apart. The heron flies with the neck folded up, while the crane keeps its neck stretched straight out. Herons build large stick nests high in trees near rivers or lakes. They are colony nesters, and often several nests may be found in the same tree.

Trumpeter Swan. The trumpeter swan is the heaviest wild bird in North America, with adult males commonly reaching 20-28 pounds. Unfortunately, the trumpeter swan also carries the distinction of being one of our rarest waterfowl. In the drought years of the 1930's, these swans dwindled to less than 100 wild birds. Since then, protection of swans in Red Rock National Wildlife Refuge (just west of Yellowstone), as well as in the parks themselves, has helped to increase swan numbers significantly. Trumpeter swans like to build their large nest mounds on old muskrat houses or small islands in shallow lakes. They incubate their four to six eggs more than one month. These showy white birds may be seen along the Madison River or on the Yellowstone River in Yellowstone's Hayden Valley. In Grand Teton, visitors may see them on Christian Pond or on Swan Lake.

American white pelicans   Photo: Jess R. Lee

Great blue heron   Photo: Franz Camenzind

Trumpeter swans   Photo: Jeff Foott

Canada Goose. Unlike some kinds of waterfowl, the Canada goose has increased in numbers over the last 50 years. One reason for the success is that this is a remarkably adaptable bird, and this adaptability may easily be seen in the parks. Canada geese may be found nesting and rearing their young along the banks of the swift Madison and Firehole Rivers, small ponds and marshes in northern Yellowstone, islands in the middle of the Snake River, and along the shores of Jackson Lake. Canada geese prefer to nest on small islands or muskrat houses, where they may more easily protect their four to eight white eggs from land predators. After the goslings hatch, they spend their first days feeding on aquatic insects and then gradually turn to grazing fresh green plant sprouts near the shore and on land. Adult geese usually pair for life, and they can be very aggressive defenders of their young.

Red-tailed Hawk. A fine summer day, with a deep blue sky and puffy white clouds, is made complete with a red-tailed hawk soaring overhead. The hawk may circle upward until it appears to be just a small speck, but it is still capable of scanning the ground for the slightest movement of a careless deer mouse, or the twitch of a ground squirrel's ear. If the hawk is lucky enough to catch his prey, the victim is promptly delivered to one to four eager young mouths back at the nest. The nest is a bushel-basket sized mass of dead sticks, usually located high in a tree along the forest edge. The same nest site may be used several years in a row by a pair of adults. Red-tailed hawks may be found almost anywhere in the parks but seem especially fond of hunting near large meadows or sagebrush flats.

Bald Eagle. Yellowstone and Grand Teton and surrounding lands comprise one of the few areas in North America where a person can actually expect to see our national bird on any given day. Good places to look for the bald eagle are along the Yellowstone, Madison, and Snake Rivers, and around Jackson and Yellowstone Lakes. Birds are concentrated here because they are protected from human harassment at nesting sites, and because their favorite foods, fish, ducks, and carrion, are abundant. Nationally, bald eagles are quite scarce. Their numbers were severely depleted when pesticides like DDT caused a reduction in egg hatching success, and now good nesting and feeding habitat is in short supply. Bald eagles do not mature until they are four to five years old, and they may produce only one or two young per year. This low reproductive rate is one reason why it will take a long time for eagle numbers to recover in North America.

Canada goose family

Red-tailed hawk

Bald eagle

Ruffed Grouse. Ruffed grouse seem to prefer a mixed forest of lodgepole pine, subalpine fir, spruce, and aspen. Usually they live on gentle slopes near the base of a mountain, and a small stream is almost always nearby. Unlike their blue grouse cousins, which migrate up and down the mountain slopes, ruffed grouse live in the same area all year. The male's life is centered around one or two large logs in the forest that are called drumming logs. In the spring, he sits on his chosen log and flaps his wings rapidly, which produces a soft thumping, or drumming sound. This display is done to attract local female grouse. The female rears a brood of eight to fourteen chicks and soon takes them to nearby meadows, where they feed on clover leaves, strawberries, and insects. When in the open, they must always be on guard for winged predators, like the goshawk.

Sage Grouse. Sage grouse live in the grassland-shrubland areas, beyond the low mountain foothills. The birds are relatively common in the sagebrush flats in the southern end of Grand Teton but are not found in Yellowstone. In spring, the male sage grouse gather in small areas, called leks, and put on their courtship displays for the hens. They inflate a large white-feathered air sack on their necks, spread their tail feathers, and drag their wings—all of which are designed to attract females. During spring and summer, the grouse eat a variety of green forbs, grasses, and shrubs. In fall and winter, the diet shifts almost exclusively to sagebrush leaves. Sometimes the birds migrate many miles to find suitable sagebrush wintering areas.

Great Horned Owl. When March winds howl and wet snow piles in four-foot drifts, it is hard to imagine any bird building a nest and laying eggs. However, the great horned owl does, and maybe the harsh environment is what makes this bird so fierce. This winged predator feeds on grouse, hares, mice, ducks, other owls, and even skunks. Fringed edging on the flight feathers helps the owls approach their quarry silently. Owls can see in very dim light but, contrary to what many people believe, they cannot see in total darkness. Experiments have shown, however, that even a blindfolded owl can use its super-sensitive ears to locate potential prey. The great horned owl is a yearlong resident at the lower elevations in both parks.

Ruffed grouse   Photo: Diana Stratton
Sage grouse   Photo: Jackie Gilmore

Great horned owl fledgling   Photo: Diana Stratton

Calliope Hummingbird. Not only do both parks offer a home to the largest bird in North America (the trumpeter swan), they also offer prime habitat for the smallest—the calliope hummingbird. Although this bird weighs considerably less than an ounce, it acts much bigger. If an animal happens to stray too close to a hummer's favorite red or blue feeding flowers, it is likely to receive a buzzing, twittering protest from the "owner," complete with power dives. The calliope hummingbird that first finds a good stand of flowers tries to defend his nectar source against others of his kind. Later in the summer, the larger rufous hummingbird often shows up and drives the calliope away to poorer pastures. Calliope hummingbirds may be seen in Yellowstone in the meadows around the Lake area developments. The Beaver Creek area in Grand Teton also attracts many hummingbirds.

Common Raven. Many biologists believe the common raven is the most intelligent bird in North America. The Blackfeet Indians called the raven "The bird that never goes hungry" because they thought it was always smart enough to find a meal somewhere. There seems to be truth in these beliefs, since ravens will find an animal within hours of its death and gather in a large flock to share in the feast. If carrion is not available, the big birds will walk in meadows searching for seed or insects or visit the rivers to see if a dead fish may have washed ashore. Ravens resemble crows, except they are about twice as large and have a ruff of feathers—the "goiter"—on the throat. Common ravens are, indeed, common in both parks and may be found all the way from sagebrush flats to alpine tundra.

Clark's Nutcracker. Taking a hike along the Teton Crest Trail in southwestern Grand Teton, or maybe the Fawn Pass Trail in northwestern Yellowstone, is a good way to see plenty of Clark's nutcrackers. As the hiker gets closer to treeline, the nutcrackers' "kerr, kerr" calls become more common. This robin-sized bird is often confused with the gray jay, but the long "ice pick" bill of the nutcracker is easy to distinguish. One of the nutcracker's favorite foods is whitebark pine nuts, and the bill is just right for extracting the seed from the tough surrounding cone. Other foods include carrion, berries, and even mice. Clark's nutcrackers prefer to live near the mountaintops year-round but turn up in trees around developed areas during winter. During this season they are common residents at Moose and Beaver Creek in Grand Teton.

Calliope hummingbird
Common raven

Clark's nutcracker

Gray Jay. In grizzly country, park rangers warn walkers to make noise when on the trail, to avoid surprising a bear. While this may work in warding off bears, it does just the opposite with gray jays. These birds are very curious and are attracted to any loud sounds they hear. This is a good strategy, because the loud sounds of animals grubbing for food, fighting, or dying can mean there might be plant or animal scraps left over for the jays to scavenge. Gray jays live in coniferous forests at medium elevations in the parks, and campers in these areas are likely to experience a "camp robber" visit. Although capable of uttering many calls, these stealthy birds are silent when they glide into camp. If the camper is not careful, anything edible and smaller than a cracker is likely to be seized and carted off by the jay to a safe hiding place.

Black-billed Magpie. The black-billed magpie is one of the most visible of our park birds because it often likes to stay within sight of the highways. This roadside vigil is not for the purpose of just watching automobiles go by, however. Instead, the magpies count on the prospect that a ground squirrel or other small mammal might be struck by a car, thus providing an easy meal. Another reason these birds are so visible is because they are inhabitants of the open grassland-shrubland plant communities and generally avoid forests. Magpies build ball-shaped stick nests which are located in the thick branches of shrubby trees. Sometimes three or four of the wastebasket-sized nests are built. Evidently this presents a sort of "shell-game" to potential predators, who hopefully will give up before they find the nest with the egg prize in it.

Mountain Chickadee. Once winter temperatures drop below zero and the northwest wind begins to screech through the canyons, it seems strange that the mountain chickadee has not left the parks and headed south. One of the smallest year-round bird residents, it seems impossible that they could find enough food to keep warm. Perhaps this is why the chickadees always seem to be on the move in the coniferous forests where they live. The members of each small flock of five to ten birds constantly call back and forth as they work their way through the foliage, searching every nook and cranny for insect eggs and larvae. When evening approaches, each bird tries to find a small bark furrow or old woodpecker hole in which to roost for the night. Mountain chickadees have almost no fear of man and will pose for close-up photos throughout both parks.

Gray jay   Photo: Willard E. Dilley

Black-billed magpie   Photo: Don Cushman

Mountain chickadee   Photo: M.D. Scott

American Dipper. The American dipper is possibly the most remarkable bird in the parks. Dippers, or ouzels as they are called locally, live along many of the small, fast streams that tumble through the mountains. Their somber gray color, which gives them excellent camouflage among the rocks where they stay, belies their wonderful abilities. Using their enormous feet and sharp claws, dippers search along the shore, looking for aquatic insects. Then, they plunge into the icy water and walk on the bottom of the rushing stream, in a submarine search for food. At times they even flap their wings underwater in order to maintain their position in the strong current. The dipper builds no ordinary nest either. It is a softball-shaped affair, composed of grasses and still-living moss, with an entrance hole in the side. A favorite nest location is on a cliff wall behind a waterfall, and the dipper flies through the cascade coming and going! Visitors from southern states who hear the dipper's sweet song may recognize its similarity to that of the mockingbird.

Mountain Bluebird. Many people assume that when lightning sets trees ablaze the forest and wildlife can only suffer. Although many trees do burn, this opens up the forest to allow other kinds of "fire follower" plants to invade. Additionally, the dead tree trunks provide homes for animals like the mountain bluebird. Near treeline one may find standing snags that have been killed by fire, harsh weather, or insects. The first birds to use these trees are woodpeckers, who drill holes for their nests. When the woodpeckers move on, the mountain bluebirds appropriate the abandoned holes for their own use. After the four to six greenish-blue eggs hatch, the nearby alpine tundra and mountain meadows make ideal places for the parents to find insect food for their hungry offspring. The high mountain nights are cold, making insects slow and easy to catch in the morning. It seems part of nature's symmetry that the mountain bluebirds arrive at the same time the beautiful blue anemone flowers of the tundra begin to bloom.

Dark-eyed Junco. Of our migratory songbirds, the dark-eyed junco is one of the first to return to the parks in spring. When warm March winds start to melt a few patches of snow here and there, small flocks of juncos may be seen scratching through the flattened brown grass, hoping to find a seed or two left over from last fall. Later in the spring juncos build a neat cup-shaped nest on the ground and line it with grasses and animal hair if they can find it. The nest with its four to six spotted eggs is well concealed under a tuft of vegetation and is usually located in mixed forest and grass-forb meadow habitat. Dark-eyed juncos are common throughout Yellowstone and Grand Teton National Parks. If disturbed, they give a "chip" call and flash their white outer tail feathers.

American dipper (ouzel)

Photo: Jeff Foott

Mountain bluebird

Photo:
Diana
Stratton

Dark-eyed junco

Photo: Jackie Gilmore

THE REPTILES

Native reptiles in the two parks include two kinds of lizards and five kinds of snakes. No turtles are thought to be permanent residents. "Cold-blooded" reptiles rely upon their environment to maintain a warm enough body temperature, so the short, cool summers and long, cold winters in the parks do not encourage the survival of many of these animals.

Western Terrestrial Garter Snake. The western terrestrial garter snake is distributed throughout the parks at lower elevations but is not commonly seen. Each year, the female produces eight to nineteen young at some time between June and September. These slender snakes are colored a mottled brown, with light stripes, and prefer to hide in tall grasses and forbs near water. When an unsuspecting mouse, grasshopper, or frog happens by, there is a chance it may become the snake's meal. Garter snakes are good swimmers and have even been known to catch small trout. They avoid the snows of winter by hibernating in rodent burrows or crevices under logs and rocks.

THE AMPHIBIANS

Amphibians, like salamanders, toads, and frogs, generally spend part of their lives in water and part on land. As with reptiles, they are "cold blooded" and find a harsh environment in the parks. They are able to hibernate in the muddy bottoms of some ponds and thus are able to survive the rigors of winter.

Spotted Frog. On a warm summer day a visit to most any beaver pond in the two parks might turn up a few spotted frogs. Those people familiar with toads and frogs might think the spotted frog looks like a cross between the two. This frog is not as chunky looking as most toads, but it has many bumps on its back, which are similar to the toad's "warts." Spotted frogs emerge from hibernation in April or May and feed on insects which frequent the water's edge. In late May or June the female frogs lay several hundred eggs at a time, loosely glued together in a mass. Within a few days, tadpoles emerge to feed on tiny plant and animal life in the water. By late August, the tadpoles have transformed into miniature new spotted frogs.

Western terrestrial garter snake   Photo: Willard E. Dilley
Spotted frog   Photo: Bryan Harry

Tiger salamander   Photo: Willard E. Dilley

THE FISH

Fish are "cold-blooded" aquatic animals. They obtain oxygen from the water through use of gills. Before the arrival of European man, many lakes and streams in the parks were fishless because of natural barriers, like waterfalls.

Cutthroat Trout. The cutthroat trout is the only trout native to Grand Teton and Yellowstone National Parks. The brook, brown, lake, and rainbow trouts, which also are found in both parks, were introduced years ago in an attempt to enhance fishing opportunities. Most fish stocking has ceased in the parks, and it is hoped that the cutthroat trout will increase in number. There are two recognized subspecies of cutthroat trout in the parks. The most widespread is the Yellowstone cutthroat, which has a yellowish-brown body with dark spots. A variety of this fish, the fine-spotted Snake River cutthroat trout, looks much like the Yellowstone cutthroat, except it has more, and smaller, spots on its sides. It lives mainly in the lower Lewis River and the Snake River. The westslope cutthroat trout subspecies is more of a silver color than the other two. It is found only in two small streams in Yellowstone.

Cutthroat trout   Photo: Robert E. Gresswell

Cutthroat trout   Photo: Willard E. Dilley

Teton Range   Photo: M. Wheelwright

APPENDIX

A CHECKLIST OF ANIMALS FOUND IN YELLOWSTONE AND GRAND TETON NATIONAL PARKS[1]

Mammals

Seasonal Status[2]	Common Name[3]	Scientific Name[3]
R	Masked shrew	*Sorex cinereus*
R	Vagrant shrew	*Sorex vagrans*
R	Montane shrew	*Sorex monticolus*
R	Dwarf shrew	*Sorex nanus*
R	Northern water shrew	*Sorex palustris*
S	Little brown bat	*Myotis lucifugus*
R	Long-eared myotis	*Myotis evotis*
S G[4]	Long-legged myotis	*Myotis volans*
R	Big brown bat	*Eptesicus fuscus*
S	Silver-haired bat	*Lasionycteris noctivagans*
S	Hoary bat	*Lasiurus cinereus*
R	Townsend's big-eared bat	*Plecotus townsendii*
R	Black bear	*Ursus americanus*
R	Grizzly bear	*Ursus arctos horribilis*
A	Raccoon	*Procyon lotor*
R	Marten	*Martes americana*
A Y	Fisher	*Martes pennanti*
R	Ermine	*Mustela erminea*
R G	Least weasel	*Mustela nivalis*
R	Long-tailed weasel	*Mustela frenata*
R	Mink	*Mustela vison*
R	Wolverine	*Gulo gulo*
R	Badger	*Taxidea taxus*
R	Striped skunk	*Mephitis mephitis*
R	River otter	*Lutra canadensis*
R	Coyote	*Canis latrans*
R	Gray wolf	*Canis lupes*
R	Red fox	*Vulpes vulpes*
R	Mountain lion	*Felis concolor*
R	Lynx	*Lynx canadensis*
R	Bobcat	*Lynx rufus*
R	Pika	*Ochotona princeps*
R	Snowshoe hare	*Lepus americanus*
R	White-tailed jack rabbit	*Lepus townsendii*
R Y	Nuttall's cottontail	*Sylvilagus nuttallii*
R	Least chipmunk	*Tamias minimus*
R	Yellow-pine chipmunk	*Tamias amoenus*
R	Uinta chipmunk	*Tamias umbrinus*
R	Yellow-bellied marmot	*Marmota flaviventris*
R	Uinta ground squirrel	*Spermophilus armatus*
R	Golden-mantled ground squirrel	*Spermophilus lateralis*
R	Red squirrel	*Tamiasciurus hudsonicus*
R	Northern flying squirrel	*Glaucomys sabrinus*
R	Northern pocket gopher	*Thomomys talpoides*
R	Beaver	*Castor canadensis*
R	Deer mouse	*Peromyscus maniculatus*
R	Bushy-tailed woodrat	*Neotoma cinerea*
R	Southern red-backed vole	*Clethrionomys gapperi*
R	Heather vole	*Phenacomys intermedius*
R	Water vole	*Microtus richardsoni*
R	Meadow vole	*Microtus pennsylvanicus*
R	Montane vole	*Microtus montanus*

R	Long-tailed vole	*Microtus longicaudus*
R G	Sagebrush vole	*Lagurus curtatus*
R	Muskrat	*Ondatra zibethicus*
R	Western jumping mouse	*Zapus princeps*
R	Porcupine	*Erethizon dorsatum*
R	Wapiti (elk)	*Cervus elaphus*
R	Mule deer	*Odocoileus hemionus*
A	White-tailed deer	*Odocoileus virginianus*
R	Moose	*Alces alces*
R	Pronghorn	*Antilocapra americana*
R	Bison (buffalo)	*Bison bison*
R	Bighorn sheep	*Ovis canadensis*
A	Mountain goat[5]	*Oreamnos americanus*

Birds

Seasonal Status	Common Name	Scientific Name
	LOONS	
A	Pacific loon	*Gavia pacifica*
M	Common loon	*Gavia immer*
	GREBES	
S	Pied-billed grebe	*Podilymbus podiceps*
S	Horned grebe	*Podiceps auritus*
M	Red-necked grebe	*Podiceps grisegena*
S	Eared grebe	*Podiceps nigricollis*
S	Western grebe	*Aechmophorus occidentalis*
A Y	Clark's grebe	*Aechmophorus clarkii*
	PELICANS	
S	American white pelican	*Pelecanus erythrorhynchos*
	CORMORANTS	
S	Double-crested cormorant	*Phalacrocorax auritus*
	HERONS, EGRETS, AND BITTERNS	
S	American bittern	*Botaurus lentiginosus*
R	Great blue heron	*Ardea herodias*
A G	Great egret	*Casmerodius albus*
S	Snowy egret	*Egretta thula*
A G	Cattle egret	*Bubulcus ibis*
A G	Green-backed heron	*Butorides striatus*
M	Black-crowned night-heron	*Nycticorax nycticorax*
	IBISES	
A	White-faced ibis	*Plegadis chihi*
	WATERFOWL	
M	Tundra swan	*Cygnus columbianus*
R	Trumpeter swan	*Cygnus buccinator*
A	Greater white-fronted goose	*Anser albifrons*
M	Snow goose	*Chen caerulescens*
A	Brant	*Branta bernicla*
R	Canada goose	*Branta canadensis*
S	Wood duck	*Aix sponsa*
R	Green-winged teal	*Anas crecca*
R	Mallard	*Anas platyrhynchos*
R	Northern pintail	*Anas acuta*
R	Blue-winged teal	*Anas discors*
R	Cinnamon teal	*Anas cyanoptera*
R	Northern shoveler	*Anas clypeata*
R	Gadwall	*Anas strepera*

R	American wigeon	*Anas americana*
A	Eurasian wigeon	*Anas penelope*
S	Canvasback	*Aythya valisineria*
S	Redhead	*Aythya americana*
R	Ring-necked duck	*Aythya collaris*
A	Greater scaup	*Aythya marila*
S	Lesser scaup	*Aythya affinis*
S	Harlequin duck	*Histrionicus histrionicus*
A G	Surf scoter	*Melanitta perspicillata*
A	White-winged scoter	*Melanitta fusca*
A Y	Black scoter	*Melanitta nigra*
R	Common goldeneye	*Bucephala clangula*
R	Barrow's goldeneye	*Bucephala islandica*
R	Bufflehead	*Bucephala albeola*
M	Hooded merganser	*Lophodytes cucullatus*
R	Common merganser	*Mergus merganser*
M	Red-breasted merganser	*Mergus serrator*
S	Ruddy duck	*Oxyura jamaicensis*

VULTURES, HAWKS, AND FALCONS

A	Turkey vulture	*Cathartes aura*
S	Osprey	*Pandion haliaetus*
A G	Black-shouldered kite	*Elanus caeruleus*
R	Bald eagle	*Haliaeetus leucocephalus*
R	Northern harrier	*Circus cyaneus*
S	Sharp-shinned hawk	*Accipiter striatus*
S	Cooper's hawk	*Accipiter cooperii*
R	Northern goshawk	*Accipiter gentilis*
A G	Broad-winged hawk	*Buteo platypterus*
S	Swainson's hawk	*Buteo swainsoni*
S	Red-tailed hawk	*Buteo jamaicensis*
S	Ferruginous hawk	*Buteo regalis*
W	Rough-legged hawk	*Buteo lagopus*
R	Golden eagle	*Aquila chrysaetos*
S	American kestrel	*Falco sparverius*
S	Merlin	*Falco columbarius*
S	Peregrine falcon	*Falco peregrinus*
A G	Gyrfalcon	*Falco rusticolus*
R	Prairie falcon	*Falco mexicanus*
A Y	Crested caracara	*Polyborus plancus*

PHEASANTS, GROUSE, AND QUAIL

R	<u>Gray partridge</u>	<u>*Perdix perdix*</u>
R G	<u>Chukar</u>	<u>*Alectoris chukar*</u>
R	Blue grouse	*Dendragapus obscurus*
R	Ruffed grouse	*Bonasa umbellus*
R G	Sage grouse	*Centrocercus urophasianus*
A G	Sharp-tailed grouse	*Tympanuchus phasianellus*

RAILS AND COOTS

A	Virginia rail	*Rallus limicola*
S	Sora	*Porzana carolina*
S	American coot	*Fulica americana*

CRANES

S	Sandhill crane	*Grus canadensis*
S	Whooping crane	*Grus americana*

PLOVERS

M	Black-bellied plover	*Pluvialis squatarola*
A G	Lesser golden-plover	*Pluvialis dominica*

M	Semipalmated plover	*Charadrius semipalmatus*
S	Killdeer	*Charadrius vociferus*
A G	Mountain plover	*Charadrius montanus*

SHOREBIRDS

A	Black-necked stilt	*Himantopus mexicanus*
S	American avocet	*Recurvirostra americana*
A Y	Ruddy turnstone	*Arenaria interpres*
S	Greater yellowlegs	*Tringa melanoleuca*
S	Lesser yellowlegs	*Tringa flavipes*
S	Solitary sandpiper	*Tringa solitaria*
S	Willet	*Catoptrophorus semipalmatus*
S	Spotted sandpiper	*Actitis macularia*
A G	Upland sandpiper	*Bartramia longicauda*
S	Long-billed curlew	*Numenius americanus*
S	Marbled godwit	*Limosa fedoa*
M G	Red knot	*Calildris canutus*
S	Sanderling	*Calidris alba*
S	Semipalmated sandpiper	*Calidris pusilla*
S G	Western sandpiper	*Calidris mauri*
S	Least sandpiper	*Calidris minutilla*
S	Baird's sandpiper	*Calidris bairdii*
M	Pectoral sandpiper	*Calidris melanotos*
A G	Dunlin	*Calidris alpina*
M G	Stilt sandpiper	*Calidris himantopus*
S	Long-billed dowitcher	*Limnodromus scolopaceus*
S	Common snipe	*Gallinago gallinago*
A G	American woodcock	*Scolopax minor*

PHALAROPES

S	Wilson's phalarope	*Phalaropus tricolor*
M	Red-necked phalarope	*Phalaropus lobatus*

JAEGERS

A G	Parasitic jaeger	*Stercorarius parasiticus*

GULLS AND TERNS

S	Franklin's gull	*Larus pipixcan*
M	Bonaparte's gull	*Larus philadelphia*
S	Ring-billed gull	*Larus delawarensis*
S	California gull	*Larus californicus*
A G	Western gull	*Larus occidentalis*
A G	Sabine's gull	*Xema sabini*
S	Caspian tern	*Sterna caspia*
S	Common tern	*Sterna hirundo*
S	Forster's tern	*Sterna forsteri*
S	Black tern	*Chlidonias niger*
A G	Ancient murrelet	*Synthliboramphus antiquus*

DOVES AND CUCKOOS

R	Rock dove	*Columba livia*
A G	Band-tailed pigeon	*Columba fasciata*
S	Mourning dove	*Zenaida macroura*
S	Black-billed cuckoo	*Coccyzus erythropthalmus*
A G	Yellow-billed cuckoo	*Coccyzus americanus*

OWLS

A G	Common barn-owl	*Tyto alba*
A G	Flammulated owl	*Otus flammeolus*
R	Western screech-owl	*Otus kennicotti*
R	Great horned owl	*Bubo virginianus*

A	Snowy owl	*Nyctea scandiaca*
A Y	Northern hawk-owl	*Surnia ulula*
R	Northern pygmy-owl	*Glaucidium gnoma*
S	Burrowing owl	*Athene cunicularia*
A	Barred owl	*Strix varia*
R	Great gray owl	*Strix nebulosa*
S	Long-eared owl	*Asio otus*
S	Short-eared owl	*Asio flammeus*
R	Boreal owl	*Aegolius funereus*
R	Northern saw-whet owl	*Aegolius acadicus*

NIGHTJARS

S	Common nighthawk	*Chordeiles minor*
S G	Common poorwill	*Phalaenoptilus nuttallii*

SWIFTS AND HUMMINGBIRDS

A Y	Black swift	*Cypseloides niger*
S	White-throated swift	*Aeronautes saxatalis*
A G	Magnificent hummingbird	*Eugenes fulgens*
S G	Black-chinned hummingbird	*Archilochus alexandri*
S	Calliope hummingbird	*Stellula calliope*
S	Broad-tailed hummingbird	*Selasphorus platycercus*
S	Rufous hummingbird	*Selasphorus rufus*

KINGFISHERS

R	Belted kingfisher	*Ceryle alcyon*

WOODPECKERS

S	Lewis' woodpecker	*Melanerpes lewis*
A	Red-headed woodpecker	*Melanerpes erythrocephalus*
A G	Acorn woodpecker	*Melanerpes formicivorus*
S	Red-naped sapsucker	*Sphyrapicus nuchalis*
S	Williamson's sapsucker	*Sphyrapicus thyroideus*
R	Downy woodpecker	*Picoides pubescens*
R	Hairy woodpecker	*Picoides villosus*
A G	White-headed woodpecker	*Picoides albolarvatus*
R	Three-toed woodpecker	*Picoides tridactylus*
R	Black-backed woodpecker	*Picoides arcticus*
R	Northern flicker	*Colaptes auratus*
A	Pileated woodpecker	*Dryocopus pileatus*

FLYCATCHERS

S	Olive-sided flycatcher	*Contopus borealis*
S	Western wood-pewee	*Contopus sordidulus*
S	Willow flycatcher	*Empidonax traillii*
A	Least flycatcher	*Empidonax minimus*
S	Hammond's flycatcher	*Empidonax hammondii*
S	Dusky flycatcher	*Empidonax oberholseri*
S	Western flycatcher	*Empidonax difficilis*
S	Say's phoebe	*Sayornis saya*
A G	Great crested flycatcher	*Myiarchus crinitus*
S	Eastern kingbird	*Tyrannus tyrannus*
S	Western kingbird	*Tyrannus verticalis*
A Y	Cassin's kingbird	*Tyrannus vociferans*

LARKS

S	Horned lark	*Eremophila alpestris*

SWALLOWS

S	Tree swallow	*Tachycineta bicolor*
S	Violet-green swallow	*Tachycineta thalassina*

S	Northern rough-winged swallow	*Steligidopteryx serripennis*
S	Bank swallow	*Riparia riparia*
S	Cliff swallow	*Hirundo pyrrhonota*
S	Barn swallow	*Hirundo rustica*

CROWS, JAYS, AND MAGPIES

R	Gray jay	*Perisoreus canadensis*
R	Steller's jay	*Cyanocitta stelleri*
A Y	Blue jay	*Cyanocitta cristata*
S	Pinyon jay	*Gymnorhinus cyanocephalus*
R	Clark's nutcracker	*Nucifraga columbiana*
R	Black-billed magpie	*Pica pica*
R	American crow	*Corvus brachyrhynchos*
R	Common Raven	*Corvus corax*

CHICKADEES

R	Black-capped chickadee	*Parus atricapillus*
R	Mountain chickadee	*Parus gambeli*
A G	Plain titmouse	*Parus inornatus*

NUTHATCHES

R	Red-breasted nuthatch	*Sitta canadensis*
R	White-breasted nuthatch	*Sitta carolinensis*
A	Pygmy nuthatch	*Sitta pygmaea*

CREEPERS

R	Brown creeper	*Certhia americana*

WRENS

R	Rock wren	*Salpinctes obsoletus*
S	House wren	*Troglodytes aedon*
S G	Winter wren	*Troglodytes troglodytes*
S	Marsh wren	*Cistothorus palustris*
A	Canyon wren	*Catherpes mexicanus*

DIPPERS

R	American dipper	*Cinclus mexicanus*

KINGLETS

R	Golden-crowned kinglet	*Regulus satrapa*
R	Ruby-crowned kinglet	*Regulus calendula*
M G	Blue-gray gnatcatcher	*Polioptila caerulea*

THRUSHES

A	Western bluebird	*Sialia mexicana*
S	Mountain bluebird	*Sialia currucoides*
R	Townsend's solitaire	*Myadestes townsendi*
S	Veery	*Catharus fuscescens*
S	Swainson's thrush	*Catharus ustulatus*
S	Hermit thrush	*Catharus guttatus*
R	American robin	*Turdus migratorius*
A	Varied thrush	*Ixoreus naevius*

MIMIC-THRUSHES

S	Gray catbird	*Dumetella carolinensis*
A G	Northern mockingbird	*Mimus polyglottos*
S	Sage thrasher	*Oreoscoptes montanus*

PIPITS

S	Water pipit	*Anthus spinoletta*
M G	Sprague's pipit	*Anthus spragueii*

WAXWINGS

R	Bohemian waxwing	*Bombycilla garrulus*
R	Cedar waxwing	*Bombycilla cedrorum*

SHRIKES

M	Northern shrike	*Lanius excubitor*
S	Loggerhead shrike	*Lanius ludovicianus*

STARLINGS

R	European starling	*Sturnus vulgaris*

VIREOS

S	Solitary vireo	*Vireo solitarius*
S	Warbling vireo	*Vireo gilvus*
S	Red-eyed vireo	*Vireo olivaceus*

WARBLERS

S	Tennessee warbler	*Vermivora peregrina*
S	Orange-crowned warbler	*Vermivora celata*
A	Nashville warbler	*Vermivora ruficapilla*
S	Yellow warbler	*Dendroica petechia*
A G	Chestnut-sided warbler	*Dendroica pensylvanica*
A G	Black-throated blue warbler	*Dendroica caerulescens*
S	Yellow-rumped warbler	*Dendroica coronata*
S	Townsend's warbler	*Dendroica townsendi*
A G	Blackburnian warbler	*Dendroica fusca*
A G	Palm warbler	*Dendroica palmarum*
A G	Bay-breasted warbler	*Dendroica castanea*
S	American redstart	*Setophaga ruticilla*
A G	Prothonotary warbler	*Protonotaria citrea*
S	Northern waterthrush	*Seiurus noveboracensis*
S	MacGillivray's warbler	*Oporonis tolmiei*
S	Common yellowthroat	*Geothlypis trichas*
S	Wilson's warbler	*Wilsonia pusilla*
S	Yellow-breasted chat	*Icteria virens*

TANAGERS

S	Western tanager	*Piranga ludoviciana*
A Y	Scarlet tanager	*Piranga olivacea*

GROSBEAKS AND BUNTINGS

M	Rose-breasted grosbeak	*Pheucticus ludovicianus*
S	Black-headed grosbeak	*Pheucticus melanocephalus*
S	Lazuli bunting	*Passerina amoena*
A	Indigo bunting	*Passerina cyanea*

NEW WORLD SPARROWS AND THEIR ALLIES

S	Green-tailed towhee	*Pipilo chlorurus*
S	Rufous-sided towhee	*Pipilo erythrophthalmus*
A G	Brown towhee	*Pipilo fuscus*
R	American tree sparrow	*Spizella arborea*
S	Chipping sparrow	*Spizella passerina*
S G	Clay-colored sparrow	*Spizella pallida*
S	Brewer's sparrow	*Spizella breweri*
S	Vesper sparrow	*Pooecetes gramineus*
S	Lark sparrow	*Chondestes grammacus*
A G	Black-throated sparrow	*Amphispiza bilineata*
A	Sage sparrow	*Amphispiza belli*
S	Lark bunting	*Calamospiza melanocorys*
S	Savannah sparrow	*Passerculus sandwichensis*
A	Grasshopper sparrow	*Ammodramus savannarum*

S	Fox sparrow	*Passerella iliaca*
R	Song sparrow	*Melospiza melodia*
S	Lincoln's sparrow	*Melospiza lincolnii*
A G	Swamp sparrow	*Melospiza Georgiana*
M	White-throated sparrow	*Zonotrichia albicollis*
S	White-crowned sparrow	*Zonotrichia leucophrys*
S	Harris' sparrow	*Zonotrichia querula*
R	Dark-eyed junco	*Junco hyemalis*
A G	McCown's longspur	*Calcarius mccownii*
A	Lapland longspur	*Calcarius lapponicus*
W	Snow bunting	*Plectrophenax nivalis*

NEW WORLD BLACKBIRDS AND ORIOLES

S	Bobolink	*Dolichonyx oryzivorus*
S	Red-winged blackbird	*Agelaius phoeniceus*
S	Western meadowlark	*Sturnella neglecta*
S	Yellow-headed blackbird	*Xanthocephalus xanthocephalus*
A G	Rusty blackbird	*Euphagus carolinus*
S	Brewer's blackbird	*Euphagus cyanocephalus*
S	Common grackle	*Quiscalus quiscula*
S	Brown-headed cowbird	*Molothrus ater*
A G	Orchard oriole	*Icterus spurius*
S	Northern oriole	*Icterus galbula*

FINCHES

R	Rosy finch	*Leucosticte arctoa*
R	Pine grosbeak	*Pinicola enucleator*
R	Cassin's finch	*Carpodacus cassinii*
A G	House finch	*Carpodacus mexicanus*
R	Red crossbill	*Loxia curvirostra*
A	White-winged crossbill	*Loxia leucoptera*
R	Common redpoll	*Carduelis flammea*
A	Hoary redpoll	*Carduelis hornemanni*
R	Pine siskin	*Carduelis pinus*
S	American goldfinch	*Carduelis tristis*
R	Evening grosbeak	*Coccothraustes vespertinus*

OLD WORLD SPARROWS

R	House sparrow	*Passer domesticus*

Reptiles

Seasonal Status	Common Name	Scientific Name
A Y	Short-horned lizard	*Phrynosoma douglassii*
R Y	Sagebrush lizard	*Sceloporus graciosus*
R	Rubber boa	*Charina bottae*
R	Bullsnake	*Pituophis catenifer*
R	Western terrestrial garter snake	*Thamnophis elegans*
R	Common garter snake	*Thamnophis sirtalis*
R Y	Western rattlesnake	*Crotalus viridis*

Amphibians

Seasonal Status	Common Name	Scientific Name
R	Tiger salamander	*Ambystoma tigrinum*
R	Western toad	*Bufo boreas*
R	Striped chorus frog	*Pseudacris triseriata*
R G[6]	Bullfrog	*Rana catesbeiana*
R	Northern leopard frog	*Rana pipiens*
R	Spotted frog	*Rana pretiosa*

Fishes

Seasonal Status	Common Name	Scientific Name
R	Mountain whitefish	*Prosopium williamsoni*
R	Brown trout	*Salmo trutta*
R	Yellowstone cutthroat trout (incl. Snake River cutthroat)	*Salmo clarki bouvieri*
R Y	Westslope cutthroat trout	*Salmo clarki lewisi*
R	Rainbow trout	*Salmo gairdneri*
R	Eastern brook trout	*Salvelinus fontinalis*
R	Lake trout	*Salvelinus namaycush*
R Y	Montana grayling	*Thymallus arcticus*
R	Utah chub	*Gila atraria*
R G	Leatherside chub	*Gila copei*
R Y	Lake chub	*Couesius plumbeus*
R	Longnose dace	*Rhinichthys cataractae*
R	Speckled dace	*Rhinichthys osculus*
R	Redside shiner	*Richardsonius balteatus*
R Y	Longnose sucker	*Catostomus catostomus*
R	Utah sucker	*Catostomus ardens*
R	Mountain sucker	*Catostomus platyrhynchus*
R G	Bluehead sucker	*Catostomus discobolus*
R	Mottled sculpin	*Cottus bairdi*
R G	Piute sculpin	*Cottus beldingi*
R G[6]	Guppy	*Poecilia reticulata*
R G[6]	Green swordtail	*Ziphophorus helleri*

[1] We thank the Resource Management staff in Grand Teton National Park for their help in assembling this list. Portions of the Yellowstone National Park bird list were obtained from: McEneaney, Terry. 1988. Birds of Yellowstone. Roberts Rinehart, Boulder, CO.

[2] R = Resident year-round; S = Summer resident only (not necessarily breeding); M = Migratory species only; W = Winter resident only; A = Accidental occurrence only.

[3] Common and scientific names follow Banks et al. 1987 and Baxter and Simon 1970 (see reference list).

[4] G = Grand Teton National Park records only.
Y = Yellowstone National Park records only.

[5] Underline denotes an introduced species.

[6] From releases in Kelly Warm Springs

REFERENCES

Bailey, V. 1930.Animal life of Yellowstone National Park. Charles C. Thomas Pub. Co., Baltimore, MD. 241 pp.

Banks, R.C., R.W. McDiarmid, and A.L. Gardner (eds.). 1987. Checklist of vertebrates of the United States, the U.S. Territories, and Canada. U.S.D.I. Fish and Wildlife Service, Wash., D.C. 79 pp.

Baxter,G.T. and J.R. Simon. 1970. Wyoming Fishes. Bull. No. 4, Wyoming Game and Fish Dept., Cheyenne, WY. 168 pp.

Baxter,G.T. and M.D.Stone. 1985. Amphibians and Reptiles of Wyoming. Wyoming Game and Fish Dept., Cheyenne, WY. 137 pp.

Burt, W.H. and R.P. Grossenheider. 1964. A field guide to the mammals. Houghton Mifflin Co., Boston, MA. 284 pp.

Chapman, J.A. and G.A. Feldhamer (eds.). 1982. Wild mammals of North America. Biology, management, and economics. Johns Hopkins Univ. Press, Baltimore, MD. 1147 pp.

Clark, T.W. and M.R. Stromberg. 1987. Mammals in Wyoming. Public Education Series No. 10. Univ. of Kansas Museum of Natural History, Lawrence, KS. 314 pp.

Negus, N.C. and J.S. Findley. 1959. Mammals of Jackson Hole, Wyoming. J. of Mammalogy 40 (3):371-381.

Oakleaf, B., H. Downing, B. Raynes, M. Raynes, and O.K. Scott. 1982. Wyoming avian atlas (with 1987 update). Wyoming Game and Fish Dept., Cheyenne, WY. 87 pp.

Shaw, R.J. 1976. Field guide to the vascular plants of Grand Teton National Park and Teton County, Wyoming. Grand Teton Natural History Assoc., Moose, WY. 301 pp.

Turner, F.B. 1955. Reptiles and amphibians of Yellowstone National Park. Yellowstone Interpretive Series No. 5, Yellowstone Library and Museum Assoc., Yellowstone National Park, WY. 40 pp.

Udvardy, M.D.F. 1977. The Audubon Society Field Guide to North American Birds, Western Region. Alfred A. Knopf, Inc., New York, NY. 854 pp.

Varley, J.D. and P. Schullery. 1983. Freshwater wilderness, Yellowstone fishes and their world. Yellowstone Library and Museum Assoc., Yellowstone National Park, WY. 132 pp.

Whitaker, J.O., Jr. 1980. The Audubon Society Field Guide to North American Mammals. Alfred A. Knopf, Inc., New York, NY. 745 pp.

INDEX

Numbers in *italics* refer to pages with photographs